# How **AI** Can **TRANSFORM YOUR BUSINESS** with Digital Marketing

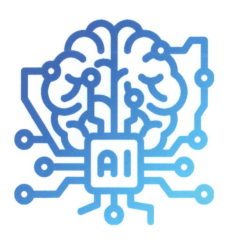

by Nicolas Fernandez Q

"To the dreamer in me and the visionary in you."

This book is dedicated to my child, a reminder that
we must embrace technology and growth. I take
these steps in the present, fully aware of the
changing world around us.
You will inherit a world brimming with knowledge
and innovation. Learn, grow, and share what you
have learned. This is the essence of progress.
Grow, not just for yourself, but for the world you
will shape.

"Those who embrace change and seek knowledge
are the architects of the future."
— Nicolás Fernández

First Edition 2024
Nicolás Fernández Quintero
Acworth - Georgia
ISBN: 9798339476030

# How AI Can Transform Your Business with Digital Marketing

**Table of Contents**

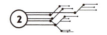

# Chapter 1:
# The Evolution of
# Digital Marketing

# From Traditional Advertising to Digital Marketing

Marketing has always been about connecting with your audience in the right place at the right time. In the past, this meant relying on traditional advertising methods like TV, radio, billboards, and print media. These methods were effective in their own right, but they lacked the precision and measurability that today's digital channels offer.

As the internet began to revolutionize the way people consume information, businesses started shifting to digital platforms. This transformation allowed companies to engage with consumers on a more personal and direct level. The rise of social media, search engines, and mobile devices opened up new possibilities for marketers to reach their audience with unprecedented accuracy.

In this new era, businesses could create tailored campaigns, track results in real-time, and adjust their strategies based on data. This digital transformation changed the game entirely, making marketing more efficient, personalized, and accessible. However, the rapid pace of technological advancement also brought its own challenges, with marketers needing to process and analyze increasingly large volumes of data.

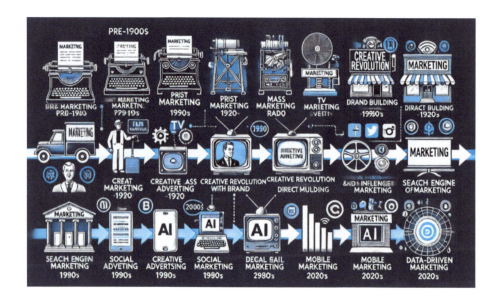

## The Role of Data in Marketing Evolution

With the rise of digital platforms, data became the cornerstone of marketing. Every interaction online—whether it's a social media like, a website visit, or an online purchase—generates data. This data helps marketers better understand their audience's behavior, preferences, and needs. As a result, companies can craft more personalized and effective campaigns.

However, managing and interpreting this vast amount of data became a daunting task for marketers. Traditional data analysis tools were no longer sufficient to handle the complexity of consumer behavior and the volume of data produced by digital interactions.

This is where Artificial Intelligence (AI) comes in. AI-powered tools allow marketers to process massive datasets in real-time, providing deeper insights that are impossible to achieve manually. AI can analyze patterns, detect trends, and predict consumer behavior, all while continually learning and improving.

## How AI Integrates Into Digital Marketing

AI has become a driving force in digital marketing because of its ability to automate processes and enhance decision-making. Here's how AI is transforming key areas of digital marketing:

1. **Personalization:** AI allows marketers to deliver highly personalized experiences at scale. By analyzing consumer data, AI can tailor content, product recommendations, and ads to individual preferences, leading to higher engagement and conversion rates.
2. **Automation:** From email marketing to social media posts, AI can automate repetitive tasks, freeing up time for marketers to focus on strategy and creativity. Automation ensures consistency and efficiency in campaign execution.
3. **Predictive Analytics:** AI can predict future consumer behavior based on historical data, allowing businesses to anticipate trends and optimize their marketing strategies. This leads to smarter decision-making and better ROI on campaigns.
4. **Customer Insights:** AI-driven tools can analyze consumer behavior across multiple touchpoints, providing valuable insights into the customer journey. This enables marketers to understand where and how to engage their audience most effectively.

# Chapter 2:
# Benefits of AI
# in Digital Marketing

As artificial intelligence (AI) continues to evolve, its integration into digital marketing has proven to be a game changer. AI enables marketers to work smarter, not harder, by automating tasks, personalizing content at scale, and analyzing vast amounts of data for better decision-making. In this chapter, we'll dive into the most significant benefits AI offers to digital marketing, helping businesses grow and succeed in today's competitive landscape.

## 1. Automation of Repetitive Processes

One of the primary advantages of AI in marketing is its ability to automate routine and time-consuming tasks. Whether it's scheduling social media posts, sending out personalized emails, or managing customer support via chatbots, AI takes care of the repetitive processes that used to consume hours of marketers' time.
AI-powered automation platforms can handle everything from:

1. **Email marketing automation:** Sending personalized emails to customers based on their behavior and preferences.
2. **Social media scheduling:** Posting content at the optimal time for engagement based on AI-driven analytics.
3. **Chatbots**: Providing real-time customer service, answering frequently asked questions, and guiding users through purchasing processes.

This automation increases efficiency, allows businesses to scale their operations, and lets marketers focus on strategy, creativity, and innovation.

As artificial intelligence (AI) continues to evolve, its integration into digital marketing has proven to be a game changer. AI enables marketers to work smarter, not harder, by automating tasks, personalizing content at scale, and analyzing vast amounts of data for better decision-making. In this chapter, we'll dive into the most significant benefits AI offers to digital marketing, helping businesses grow and succeed in today's competitive landscape.

## 1. Automation of Repetitive Processes

One of the primary advantages of AI in marketing is its ability to automate routine and time-consuming tasks. Whether it's scheduling social media posts, sending out personalized emails, or managing customer support via chatbots, AI takes care of the repetitive processes that used to consume hours of marketers' time.
AI-powered automation platforms can handle everything from:

1. **Email marketing automation:** Sending personalized emails to customers based on their behavior and preferences.
2. **Social media scheduling:** Posting content at the optimal time for engagement based on AI-driven analytics.
3. **Chatbots**: Providing real-time customer service, answering frequently asked questions, and guiding users through purchasing processes.

This automation increases efficiency, allows businesses to scale their operations, and lets marketers focus on strategy, creativity, and innovation.

## 2. Personalization at Scale

Consumers today expect personalized experiences. AI enables marketers to deliver this personalization at a scale that would be impossible to achieve manually. By analyzing user behavior, preferences, and interactions across various channels, AI can segment audiences and deliver tailored content, recommendations, and ads.
For instance:

- Product recommendations: AI analyzes customer browsing and purchase history to offer personalized product suggestions, increasing the likelihood of conversion.
- Dynamic ads: AI ensures that each user sees ads most relevant to their needs and interests, maximizing engagement.
- Website personalization: AI can adjust website content in real-time based on a user's previous interactions, creating a more customized browsing experience.

This level of personalization drives higher engagement, improves user experience, and ultimately leads to more sales.

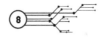

## 4. Improved Efficiency and Cost Savings

AI dramatically improves operational efficiency by automating labor-intensive tasks, streamlining processes, and optimizing resource allocation. This increased efficiency often leads to significant cost savings, especially in areas like advertising, content creation, and customer service.

For example:

- Ad spend optimization: AI-powered tools continuously monitor and adjust ad campaigns to ensure the best use of advertising budgets, targeting only the most relevant audience segments.
- Customer service automation: AI-driven chatbots reduce the need for large customer support teams, providing 24/7 service at a fraction of the cost.
- Content creation: AI can generate content like product descriptions, social media posts, and even full articles, saving time and reducing the need for human intervention in repetitive content production.

By leveraging AI, businesses can reduce overhead while simultaneously enhancing the quality of their marketing efforts.

## 5. Enhancing Customer Experience

AI plays a pivotal role in improving the overall customer experience. Through chatbots, personalized product recommendations, and predictive insights, AI creates a seamless and more enjoyable experience for users. Here's how AI enhances customer interactions:

- AI-powered chatbots: Available 24/7, these bots can answer common queries, assist in the purchase process, and provide immediate support, all without human intervention.

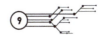

- Proactive support: AI can predict customer issues based on browsing patterns or previous interactions and offer solutions before the customer even asks.
- Personalized journeys: Every customer's journey is unique, and AI helps tailor this journey by recommending products, adjusting website content, and personalizing marketing messages based on individual preferences.

When customers feel understood and valued, their loyalty to a brand increases, leading to higher retention rates and more positive word-of-mouth.

AI not only transforms how businesses operate internally but also revolutionizes how they engage with customers, optimize their marketing efforts, and make strategic decisions. These benefits provide businesses with a competitive edge, allowing them to innovate faster and offer more tailored, efficient marketing solutions.

# Chapter 3:
# AI and Data Analytics

Data is the fuel that powers digital marketing, and with the immense growth of online platforms, businesses now have more data than ever before. However, collecting vast amounts of data is just the beginning. To truly make data actionable and beneficial for marketing strategies, it needs to be analyzed, interpreted, and transformed into insights. This is where Artificial Intelligence (AI) becomes invaluable, offering businesses the tools to optimize their data analytics and make smarter marketing decisions.

(Note to the reader: While AI is powerful, it's crucial to remember that the expertise of professionals in the field remains essential, especially when navigating complex AI-driven strategies. If you need professional support, do not hesitate to reach out to me for expert guidance in AI integration for your business.)

## How AI Optimizes Data Analysis

AI is capable of processing enormous volumes of data far faster than any human analyst could. Traditional methods of data analysis are often manual, slow, and prone to human error, while AI streamlines the entire process and enhances accuracy. With AI tools, marketers can analyze customer behavior in real-time, monitor campaign performance, and detect trends instantly.

Some key benefits of AI in data analysis include:

- Real-time data processing: AI-driven tools can analyze data as it's being generated, allowing marketers to adjust campaigns on the fly to maximize effectiveness.
- Pattern recognition: AI identifies hidden patterns within data that humans might overlook, helping businesses make better predictions and uncover opportunities.
- Sentiment analysis: AI can analyze social media posts, customer reviews, and other user-generated content to determine public sentiment toward a brand, product, or service.

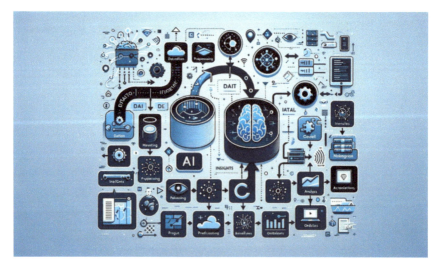

## Advanced Audience Segmentation

One of the most important aspects of successful digital marketing is reaching the right audience. AI takes audience segmentation to the next level by breaking down consumer groups into highly specific segments based on their behavior, preferences, demographics, and past interactions.

Traditional segmentation methods often categorize customers based on broad factors like age or location. However, AI enables more precise segmentation by:

- Analyzing behavior: AI can track a customer's online activity—what they click on, how they navigate a website, and what products they view or purchase—allowing businesses to create highly relevant segments.
- Predicting preferences: AI can predict what types of products or content a customer is likely to be interested in based on their previous behavior.
- Real-time adjustments: AI can update segments in real-time as new data comes in, ensuring that businesses are always targeting the most relevant audience groups.

This level of segmentation helps businesses create hyper-targeted marketing campaigns, which results in higher engagement and conversion rates.

(Image suggestion: A visual representation of customer segments, with AI highlighting key characteristics for each group.)

## Predicting Consumer Behavior

AI doesn't just help businesses understand their current customers—it also predicts future behavior, which can be a game changer for marketing strategies. Using historical data, AI algorithms can predict what actions a customer is likely to take next, such as making a purchase, engaging with a specific type of content, or even leaving the brand.

Predictive analytics can be used for:

- Predicting churn: AI can analyze user activity to identify customers who are at risk of leaving, allowing businesses to implement retention strategies before it's too late.
- Forecasting sales trends: AI can predict upcoming shifts in consumer demand, helping businesses adjust their inventory and marketing efforts accordingly.
- Optimizing product recommendations: By analyzing past purchases and browsing habits, AI can make personalized product suggestions, increasing the chances of conversion.

## Predictive Models for Marketing Campaigns

AI not only predicts consumer behavior but also helps optimize future marketing campaigns. With predictive models, marketers can make data-driven decisions on campaign elements like timing, content, and target audience. By leveraging AI, businesses can predict:

- Campaign success rates: AI can evaluate various elements of past campaigns to predict how future campaigns will perform, suggesting adjustments to improve results.
- Optimal timing for outreach: AI can analyze user engagement data to determine the best times to send marketing emails, post on social media, or run ads.
- Best-performing content types: By analyzing consumer preferences and behavior, AI can help marketers identify the types of content that are most likely to resonate with their audience.

This ability to predict outcomes allows businesses to optimize their marketing budgets and focus their resources on strategies with the highest likelihood of success.

## The Human Touch in AI-Driven Data Analytics

While AI provides incredible tools to streamline and optimize data analytics, it's important to remember that human expertise remains essential. AI can provide the data and even suggest strategies, but interpreting those insights and crafting a cohesive, creative marketing strategy requires a human touch.

As AI becomes more embedded in marketing, businesses need professionals who understand both AI and marketing strategy to ensure the tools are used to their full potential. If you ever find yourself needing expert assistance to navigate this intersection, don't hesitate to reach out to me for personalized support.

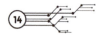

# Chapter 4: Automating Marketing with AI

One of the most significant advantages of AI in digital marketing is its ability to automate repetitive and time-consuming tasks. Automation doesn't just save time—it enhances precision, consistency, and scalability. AI-driven marketing automation tools empower businesses to deliver personalized experiences at scale while freeing up valuable time for marketers to focus on strategy and creativity.

(Note to the reader: While automation is becoming more efficient, it's important to ensure that your AI-driven marketing efforts are guided by a professional who understands how to integrate these tools effectively into your strategy. Feel free to reach out to me for expert assistance in getting started or optimizing your AI automation tools.)

## Marketing Automation Platforms and Their Benefits

AI-powered marketing automation platforms allow businesses to streamline their marketing efforts by automating processes like email campaigns, social media posts, and even customer segmentation. These platforms use machine learning to analyze consumer behavior and adjust campaigns in real time, ensuring that messages are always relevant and timely.

The primary benefits of using AI-driven marketing automation platforms include:
- Consistency: AI ensures that all marketing efforts are executed with precision and consistency across channels.
- Scalability: Automation allows businesses to scale their efforts quickly, managing more campaigns and audience segments without increasing the workload.
- Real-time adaptability: AI can adjust campaigns in real time based on performance data, optimizing outcomes without manual intervention.
- Improved ROI: With AI-driven insights and automation, businesses can achieve better results from their marketing campaigns, leading to higher returns on investment.

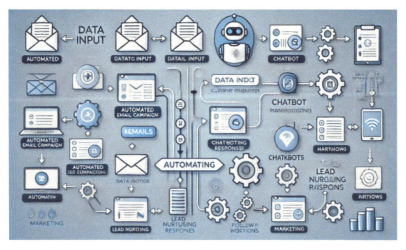

## Email, Chatbots, and Automated Customer Service

One of the most widespread uses of AI in marketing is in customer communication, particularly through automated email campaigns, chatbots, and customer service tools. AI-driven communication tools provide businesses with the ability to engage with customers 24/7 and deliver timely, personalized messages.

## Email Automation

AI takes email marketing to the next level by enabling highly personalized and dynamic campaigns. Instead of sending the same message to an entire email list, AI-driven platforms can create tailored emails based on user behavior, preferences, and past interactions. For example, AI can:

- Send personalized product recommendations based on browsing history.
- Deliver tailored offers to customers who have abandoned their shopping carts.
- Automatically send follow-up emails based on a customer's previous actions.

These personalized emails lead to higher engagement rates and increased conversions.

## AI-Powered Chatbots

AI-powered chatbots can handle customer inquiries, assist with transactions, and provide support, all without human intervention. These chatbots are capable of:
- Answering frequently asked questions.
- Guiding users through the purchasing process.
- Offering product recommendations based on user preferences.

Chatbots not only improve customer service but also free up human agents to handle more complex tasks, making operations more efficient.
(Image suggestion: A chatbot interacting with a customer, answering questions, and guiding them through a purchasing process.)

### Workflow Automation and Content Personalization

One of the most powerful features of AI in marketing is its ability to automate workflows and personalize content for individual users. AI can analyze customer data in real-time and adjust marketing messages based on their preferences and behavior, ensuring that each interaction feels tailored and relevant.

## Automated Workflows

AI allows marketers to automate entire workflows, from the initial contact with a lead to nurturing them through the sales funnel. These workflows might include:

- Triggering email sequences based on a customer's actions, such as signing up for a newsletter or downloading a resource.
- Automatically moving leads to the next stage of the sales funnel when they meet certain criteria (e.g., visiting a pricing page).
- Personalizing follow-up messages based on customer engagement and behavior.

This level of automation ensures that every customer receives the right message at the right time, helping businesses nurture leads and close sales more efficiently.

## Personalized Content Delivery

AI also enables businesses to deliver personalized content across all marketing channels, from websites to social media. By analyzing user data, AI can determine the types of content each customer is most likely to engage with, allowing businesses to:
- Display personalized website content based on user behavior and preferences.
- Tailor social media posts to individual users' interests.
- Deliver dynamic ads that change in real-time to reflect the user's interests.

This kind of personalization leads to higher engagement, better user experiences, and, ultimately, more conversions.

### The Future of Automated Marketing

The potential for AI-driven marketing automation is vast. As AI continues to improve, we can expect even more advanced tools that will automate complex marketing strategies with minimal human intervention. In the near future, AI could handle everything from content creation to complete campaign management, allowing businesses to run highly sophisticated marketing efforts without the need for constant oversight.

That said, we aren't fully there yet. As powerful as AI is, it still requires human expertise to design and monitor marketing strategies, ensuring that automation aligns with overall business goals. If you're looking to harness the power of AI in your marketing efforts but need guidance on how to get started or optimize your tools, I'm here to help. Remember, while automation will someday be fully self-sufficient, for now, we're learning to walk in this exciting new world of AI-driven marketing.

# Chapter 5:
# Content Creation
# with AI

Content is the backbone of any successful digital marketing strategy. Whether it's a blog post, social media update, video, or advertisement, creating engaging and relevant content is key to attracting and retaining customers. However, generating high-quality content consistently can be time-consuming and resource-intensive. This is where AI comes into play. With AI-powered tools, businesses can produce and optimize content at scale, making content creation faster, more efficient, and even more personalized.

(Note to the reader: While AI can generate impressive content, it's essential to ensure that the final product aligns with your brand's voice and goals. If you need professional help to fine-tune your content or ensure the right strategies are in place, feel free to reach out to me for expert guidance. Remember, the human touch is still crucial in crafting compelling and authentic content.)

## AI-Generated SEO-Optimized Content

Search engine optimization (SEO) is vital for ensuring that your content ranks well on search engines like Google. AI tools like GPT models (the very technology powering this book) can generate SEO-optimized content that meets both search engine requirements and the needs of your audience. These AI tools can analyze:

- **Keyword relevance:** AI can suggest keywords and phrases that are most likely to drive traffic based on current trends and search behavior.
- **Content structure:** AI can recommend the ideal structure for blog posts, articles, or web pages to maximize SEO performance, ensuring that the content is well-organized and easy to read.
- **Competitor analysis:** AI can assess competitor content and highlight gaps that your business can fill with unique, value-added content.

By leveraging AI to create SEO-friendly content, businesses can improve their search rankings and increase visibility online.

## Producing Images and Videos with AI

Creating high-quality visuals for your marketing campaigns can be a time-consuming process. However, AI has made it possible to produce engaging images and videos quickly and efficiently. Here's how AI can assist in visual content creation:

- **Image generation:** Tools like DALL-E and other AI-driven platforms can generate unique images based on text prompts, helping marketers create visuals that fit their specific needs without relying on stock photography.
- **Video creation:** AI-powered tools can now generate video content, from simple explainer videos to more complex animations. These tools can automatically edit footage, add effects, and optimize the video for different platforms.
- **Visual optimization:** AI can also enhance existing images and videos by optimizing them for different devices, platforms, or audiences. For example, AI can resize images for social media platforms, improve resolution, or suggest edits to improve visual appeal.

By integrating AI into your visual content strategy, you can produce eye-catching, relevant visuals faster and at a lower cost.

## Creating Effective Advertising Campaigns

Advertising is one of the most important tools in digital marketing, and AI has transformed how ads are created, targeted, and optimized. AI-driven tools can help businesses create more effective ads by:

- **Copywriting for ads:** AI can generate persuasive ad copy based on the desired tone, audience, and goal. By analyzing successful ads, AI tools can suggest headline variations, calls to action, and copy improvements.

- **Dynamic ad creation:** AI can produce dynamic ads that automatically adjust based on the user's behavior, preferences, and location. This real-time personalization increases engagement and conversion rates.
- **Ad targeting:** AI allows for precise targeting by analyzing user data to determine the best audience for each ad. This means your ads reach the right people at the right time, maximizing your return on ad spend (ROAS).
- **A/B testing:** AI tools can conduct A/B testing of ads, automatically adjusting the best-performing version in real-time to optimize results.

## Streamlining Content Creation for Social Media

Social media marketing requires a constant flow of content to keep audiences engaged. AI-powered tools can help streamline this process by automating content creation and scheduling. Here's how:

- **Content suggestions:** AI tools can analyze trending topics and suggest relevant content ideas, helping businesses stay timely and engaging.
- **Automated scheduling:** AI-driven platforms can schedule social media posts at optimal times, based on user engagement data, ensuring that content reaches the maximum number of followers.
- **Social media graphics:** AI can generate social media-friendly images, including branded templates, infographics, and promotional graphics, saving time for busy marketing teams.

With AI, businesses can maintain a steady stream of high-quality social media content without overwhelming their marketing teams.

# AI-Driven Copywriting Tools

In addition to visuals, AI can also assist with written content creation. AI-driven copywriting tools can generate compelling headlines, product descriptions, emails, and social media posts, freeing up time for marketers to focus on higher-level strategy. Some of the key benefits of AI in copywriting include:

- **Speed:** AI can generate copy in seconds, allowing marketers to quickly iterate on different versions of the same message.
- **Consistency:** AI ensures that the tone and style of the content remain consistent across multiple platforms and campaigns.
- **Personalization:** AI can tailor copy to individual users based on their preferences and behavior, making marketing messages more relevant and engaging.

## The Human Touch in AI-Generated Content

While AI can generate content quickly and efficiently, it's important to remember that the human touch is still essential. AI tools are incredibly useful for automating repetitive tasks and generating ideas, but fine-tuning the content to fit a brand's unique voice and message requires human oversight. Additionally, humans are still better at understanding emotional nuance, cultural context, and creativity—areas where AI continues to develop.

If you're looking to create AI-driven content but want to ensure it aligns with your brand and resonates with your audience, don't hesitate to reach out to me for professional assistance. AI is a powerful tool, but combining it with human expertise will lead to even better results.

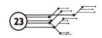

# Chapter 6: Targeted and Personalized Advertising

In the world of digital marketing, reaching the right audience with the right message at the right time is critical. AI has revolutionized how businesses can target and personalize their advertising efforts, making them more efficient, relevant, and ultimately more successful. AI allows marketers to create hyper-targeted ad campaigns that are customized for individual users based on their behavior, interests, and demographics.

(Note to the reader: As powerful as AI is in creating personalized ad campaigns, remember that a professional's guidance is invaluable. If you need assistance in designing, running, or optimizing your AI-driven ad campaigns, feel free to reach out to me. Together, we can ensure that your advertising efforts hit the mark.)

## AI-Powered Programmatic Advertising

Programmatic advertising refers to the use of AI to automate the buying and placement of ads in real-time. This method allows marketers to target specific audiences more effectively while optimizing the performance of ad spend. AI-driven programmatic platforms analyze user behavior and engagement data to make instant decisions about where and when to place ads, ensuring that every dollar is used efficiently.

Benefits of programmatic advertising with AI include:

- **Precision targeting:** AI ensures that ads are shown to the right audience based on factors such as browsing history, interests, and previous interactions with the brand.
- **Real-time bidding:** AI can automatically bid for ad space in real-time, ensuring that businesses pay the optimal price for each ad placement.
- **Cost efficiency:** By optimizing bids and placements, AI reduces wasted ad spend and ensures that marketing budgets are used effectively.

## AI-Based Audience Segmentation and Targeting

Traditional audience segmentation methods often group people into broad categories based on age, gender, location, or interests. However, AI can take segmentation to a whole new level by analyzing vast amounts of data to create micro-segments of users with similar behaviors, preferences, and tendencies.

With AI, marketers can segment audiences based on:

- Behavioral data: AI analyzes how users interact with your website, products, or content to create segments based on their actions.
- Psychographic data: AI can identify users' values, attitudes, and interests, allowing marketers to tailor ads to resonate with their personal motivations.
- Geographic data: AI allows for hyper-local targeting, ensuring that ads are relevant to users in specific locations or regions.

This precise targeting leads to more relevant ads, which in turn generates higher engagement and better conversion rates.

## Real-Time Ad Personalization

AI allows businesses to create dynamic, personalized ads that adapt in real time to the user's behavior. This level of personalization ensures that each user sees the ad content most relevant to them, whether it's a product recommendation, a tailored offer, or personalized messaging.

Some of the ways AI personalizes ads include:
- Product recommendations: AI can display personalized product suggestions in ads based on a user's previous interactions with your website or app.
- Dynamic ad content: AI can automatically adjust the content of ads to reflect the user's interests, location, or stage in the buying journey.
- Retargeting: AI can recognize users who have previously visited your site but didn't complete a purchase, serving them tailored ads to encourage them to return and complete their transaction.

## Measuring and Optimizing Ad Campaigns with AI

One of the greatest advantages of AI in advertising is its ability to constantly measure and optimize campaigns. AI can analyze ad performance in real-time and make adjustments automatically to improve results. This might include shifting budget to higher-performing ads, adjusting targeting based on new data, or changing creative elements to increase engagement.

AI tools can help marketers optimize:
- Ad placement: AI determines the best times and platforms to display ads, ensuring maximum visibility and engagement.
- Ad creative: AI can analyze which ad creatives perform best, automatically testing different versions (A/B testing) and selecting the one that drives the highest engagement.
- Budget allocation: AI continuously monitors campaign performance and reallocates budget in real-time to the ads or channels with the highest return on investment.

With AI, marketers no longer need to manually adjust campaigns; the system continually fine-tunes ads for optimal performance.

## The Future of Personalized Advertising

As AI continues to evolve, the future of personalized advertising will likely become even more advanced. AI is expected to enable deeper levels of personalization, with ads that not only reflect a user's preferences and behavior but also anticipate their needs and desires. This could include:

- **Predictive advertising:** AI will predict what products or services a user is likely to need next, serving ads that match their future needs based on past behavior.
- **Emotion-based ads:** AI could analyze a user's emotional state through facial recognition or voice analysis, serving ads that resonate with their current mood or mindset.
- **Interactive ads:** AI could power interactive ads that engage users in real time, allowing them to customize their experience or explore products in a more immersive way.

While AI will undoubtedly continue to advance, remember that expert oversight is essential to ensure that these technologies are used effectively and ethically. If you need guidance on how to stay ahead of these developments, feel free to reach out to me.

# Chapter 7:
# AI in Social Media

Social media has become a cornerstone of digital marketing, providing businesses with direct access to billions of users worldwide. With such a vast audience, the challenge lies in optimizing content, understanding trends, and engaging with users effectively. AI has made it easier for businesses to not only analyze social media behavior but also to automate tasks, enhance personalization, and boost overall performance.

### Optimizing Social Media Posts and Scheduling

Timing is everything when it comes to social media. Posting at the right time can significantly impact engagement, reach, and visibility. AI tools analyze user behavior, engagement trends, and platform algorithms to determine the optimal times to post content for maximum impact. These tools also automate the scheduling process, ensuring consistency in your social media presence.

Key benefits of using AI for social media scheduling include:
- **Optimal posting times:** AI tools can analyze when your audience is most active and automatically schedule posts for those times.
- **Content recommendations:** AI can suggest the best types of content (videos, images, polls, etc.) to post based on current trends and audience preferences.
- **Multi-platform management:** AI allows marketers to schedule and manage posts across multiple social media platforms from a single dashboard, saving time and increasing efficiency.

### Analyzing Trends and Behavior on Social Platforms

Social media platforms generate vast amounts of data every second, and AI helps marketers make sense of it all. AI-powered social listening tools can track conversations, hashtags, and mentions of your brand, providing valuable insights into what your audience is talking about and how they feel about your brand.
Some key AI applications in trend analysis and social listening include:

- **Sentiment analysis:** AI can analyze the tone of social media posts to determine whether conversations about your brand are positive, negative, or neutral.
- **Hashtag monitoring:** AI can track trending hashtags in real-time, giving marketers the ability to join relevant conversations and increase brand visibility.
- **Audience behavior insights:** AI can identify patterns in user behavior, such as which types of content drive the most engagement, helping businesses adjust their strategies accordingly.

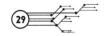

## How AI Influences User Engagement

Engaging with users on social media is essential for building a strong online presence. However, manually responding to comments, messages, and mentions can be overwhelming, especially as your audience grows. AI-powered chatbots and automation tools can handle many of these interactions, ensuring that your brand remains responsive and engaged with users at all times.

AI can enhance user engagement by:

- **Automating responses:** AI-driven chatbots can answer frequently asked questions, respond to comments, and even assist users with customer service inquiries, improving response times and customer satisfaction.
- **Personalizing interactions:** AI can analyze user data to personalize responses, making interactions feel more genuine and tailored to each individual.
- **Tracking engagement:** AI tools can track how users interact with your social media content, providing insights into which posts generate the most likes, shares, and comments.

While AI can manage many routine interactions, it's important to strike a balance between automation and human engagement, ensuring that your brand's voice remains authentic.

## The Role of AI in Influencer Marketing

- Influencer marketing has become a powerful strategy for reaching new audiences, and AI is helping businesses identify the right influencers to partner with. AI tools can analyze influencer profiles to determine their relevance, engagement rates, and audience demographics, making it easier for brands to select influencers who align with their goals.

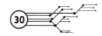

Some of the ways AI enhances influencer marketing include:

- Identifying micro and macro influencers: AI can sort through thousands of influencer profiles to find the best fit for your brand, whether you're looking for niche micro-influencers or large-scale macro influencers.
- Analyzing influencer performance: AI can track the performance of influencer campaigns in real-time, helping businesses determine whether their partnerships are driving the desired results.
- Predicting campaign outcomes: AI tools can analyze past influencer campaigns to predict how future partnerships might perform, giving businesses confidence in their influencer strategy.

## AI for Content Moderation and Social Media Management

As your social media presence grows, so does the need for content moderation. AI can help manage and moderate social media content by automatically flagging inappropriate or harmful posts and comments. This ensures that your social media platforms remain safe and welcoming for all users.

AI-powered moderation tools can:

- Detect inappropriate content: AI can automatically detect and flag offensive language, hate speech, or inappropriate content in comments and posts, ensuring a safe environment for your audience.
- **Automate comment filtering:** AI can filter out spam and irrelevant comments, making it easier for social media managers to focus on meaningful interactions.
- **Monitor brand reputation:** AI tools can track mentions of your brand across social platforms, alerting you to potential PR issues or crises before they escalate.

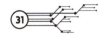

# Chapter 8: Improving Customer Experience with AI

In today's highly competitive market, customer experience (CX) has become one of the most important factors in building brand loyalty and driving growth. Artificial Intelligence (AI) is playing a key role in transforming customer interactions, enabling businesses to offer seamless, personalized, and efficient experiences across all touchpoints. From 24/7 chatbots to personalized product recommendations, AI enhances how businesses engage with customers, making interactions faster, more responsive, and more tailored to individual needs.

(Note to the reader: As AI-driven customer experience tools evolve, professional guidance can help you ensure that these tools are implemented effectively. If you need support in optimizing your AI for customer service, feel free to consult an expert in the field—such as myself—for personalized assistance.)

## AI-Powered Chatbots for 24/7 Customer Support

One of the most transformative uses of AI in customer experience is through AI-powered chatbots. These bots can handle a wide range of customer queries, from answering frequently asked questions to assisting with transactions. Unlike human agents, AI chatbots are available 24/7, providing instant responses to customer inquiries at any time of the day or night.

Some key benefits of AI chatbots include:
- **Immediate responses:** Chatbots can provide instant answers to common customer questions, improving response times and customer satisfaction.
- **Handling multiple conversations:** AI-powered chatbots can manage multiple customer interactions simultaneously, making them highly efficient during busy periods.
- **Learning over time:** With machine learning capabilities, AI chatbots become smarter over time, improving their ability to handle more complex queries and offering better responses with each interaction.

By incorporating AI chatbots into your customer service strategy, businesses can ensure that customers always have access to support when they need it, without the need for a large customer service team.

## Personalized Customer Journeys

Today's customers expect personalized experiences. AI enables businesses to provide highly customized journeys for each user based on their behavior, preferences, and past interactions. This personalized approach increases customer satisfaction and helps businesses build stronger relationships with their audience.

AI enhances personalization in several ways:
- **Tailored recommendations:** AI can analyze user data to recommend products or services that align with their preferences, increasing the likelihood of a purchase.
- **Custom content:** AI-driven algorithms can personalize the content a customer sees, such as articles, videos, or promotions, based on their interests and previous interactions with your brand.
- **Dynamic website experiences:** AI can adjust website elements in real-time to cater to each customer, such as displaying specific products or offers that are relevant to their current behavior.

This level of personalization creates a smoother, more engaging experience for customers, ultimately leading to higher conversions and improved customer loyalty.

## Predictive Analytics for Proactive Support

AI doesn't just respond to customer inquiries—it can also predict customer needs and provide proactive support. By analyzing user behavior and data, AI tools can anticipate potential issues or needs before the customer even reaches out. This proactive approach enhances the customer experience by addressing problems early and providing timely solutions.

Some examples of predictive AI in customer experience include:
- **Predicting churn:** AI can identify customers who are at risk of leaving by analyzing engagement patterns and behaviors. Businesses can then proactively offer support, discounts, or incentives to retain them.
- **Anticipating product needs:** AI can predict when customers might need to reorder a product or service based on their purchase history, allowing businesses to send timely reminders or offers.
- **Real-time issue resolution:** AI can monitor customer interactions in real-time, identifying pain points or areas of friction and offering solutions immediately.

By leveraging predictive analytics, businesses can enhance the customer experience by resolving issues before they escalate and anticipating customer needs more effectively.

## AI-Powered Product Recommendations

One of the most effective uses of AI in improving the customer experience is through product recommendations. AI analyzes customer data, including browsing behavior,

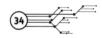

purchase history, and preferences, to offer personalized product suggestions that are highly relevant to each individual. This not only improves the shopping experience but also increases the likelihood of a purchase.

Benefits of AI-powered product recommendations include:
- **Increased sales:** Personalized recommendations based on a customer's previous interactions lead to higher conversion rates.
- **Enhanced user experience:** Customers appreciate relevant product suggestions, making their shopping experience more enjoyable and efficient.
- **Cross-selling and up-selling:** AI can suggest complementary or higher-value products based on what the customer is already viewing or purchasing, increasing the average order value.

## Real-Time Customer Feedback Analysis

Collecting and analyzing customer feedback is crucial for improving products and services, but manually sorting through surveys, reviews, and social media comments can be overwhelming. AI simplifies this process by automatically analyzing customer feedback in real-time, identifying key trends and areas for improvement.

AI tools can:
- Analyze sentiment: AI can determine whether feedback is positive, neutral, or negative, allowing businesses to quickly address customer concerns.
- Identify common themes: AI can highlight recurring topics in customer feedback, such as product issues or areas of dissatisfaction, enabling businesses to make data-driven improvements.
- Provide actionable insights: By analyzing feedback across multiple channels, AI provides businesses with clear insights on how to improve their offerings and enhance customer satisfaction.

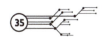

## The Balance Between Automation and Human Interaction

While AI has revolutionized the customer experience by automating many processes, it's important to strike a balance between automation and human interaction. Some customer issues require a personal touch, and there will always be scenarios where human intervention is necessary. Businesses should aim to use AI to handle routine tasks and inquiries while ensuring that human agents are available for more complex or sensitive issues.

AI has the power to enhance every aspect of the customer experience, from offering personalized recommendations to providing 24/7 support through chatbots. While AI offers numerous benefits, it's essential to complement these tools with human oversight to ensure a balanced and empathetic customer service strategy.

AI has the power to enhance every aspect of the customer experience, from offering personalized recommendations to providing 24/7 support through chatbots. While AI offers numerous benefits, it's essential to complement these tools with human oversight to ensure a balanced and empathetic customer service strategy.

# Chapter 9:
# AI Tools for
# Digital Marketing

As AI continues to transform the digital marketing landscape, numerous AI-powered tools have emerged to help businesses streamline their processes, enhance customer engagement, and optimize their campaigns. These tools cater to different aspects of marketing, from content creation and social media management to customer service and advertising. In this chapter, we will explore some of the most popular AI tools that businesses can use to take their digital marketing efforts to the next level.

(Note to the reader: While AI tools are highly effective, selecting the right one for your business can be challenging. If you need help choosing or integrating AI tools into your marketing strategy, consulting with a professional is a great way to ensure success.)

## AI Tools for Content Creation

Creating engaging content consistently can be one of the most time-consuming aspects of digital marketing. AI tools make content creation faster and more efficient by automating the process while still maintaining quality.

Some popular AI-powered content creation tools include:
- GPT-3 (OpenAI): GPT-3 is an AI language model that can generate human-like text for blog posts, articles, and even emails. It's perfect for businesses looking to scale content creation quickly.
- Jarvis (Jasper AI): This AI writing assistant helps marketers generate high-quality copy for blogs, emails, social media posts, and more. Jarvis can also optimize content for SEO, making it easier to rank higher on search engines.
- Grammarly: Grammarly is an AI-powered tool that helps improve the clarity and quality of written content by providing grammar and style suggestions.

## AI Tools for Advertising and Ad Optimization

AI has become a game-changer in advertising by making ad targeting, optimization, and bidding more efficient. AI tools can automatically adjust campaigns based on performance, helping businesses get the most out of their advertising budgets.

Some top AI advertising tools include:
- **Adext AI:** This AI-powered ad management tool automates the process of creating, targeting, and optimizing ads across platforms like Google and Facebook.
- **Revealbot:** Revealbot automates ad campaign management for Facebook and Google, using AI to optimize bids, budgets, and targeting in real-time.
- **Albert AI:** Albert is an AI marketing platform that autonomously creates and optimizes digital campaigns, including paid search, social media, and programmatic advertising.

## AI Tools for Customer Service and Chatbots

Customer service is one of the most critical areas where AI can make a significant impact. AI-powered chatbots and support systems can handle routine inquiries, freeing up human agents to focus on more complex issues.

Some popular AI-powered customer service tools include:
- **Zendesk AI:** Zendesk's AI-powered chatbot assists businesses in handling customer inquiries, providing quick responses and resolving issues efficiently.
- **Intercom:** Intercom offers AI-driven customer communication tools that include chatbots, email marketing, and customer data tracking, allowing businesses to provide personalized support at scale.
- **Drift:** Drift uses AI to automate customer conversations on websites, qualifying leads, answering questions, and offering support.

## AI Tools for Email Marketing

Email marketing remains one of the most effective channels for reaching customers, and AI tools can make it even more efficient by automating campaign creation, segmentation, and personalization.

Some useful AI tools for email marketing include:
- Mailchimp: Mailchimp uses AI to suggest the best time to send emails, personalize content, and optimize subject lines for higher open rates.
- ActiveCampaign: ActiveCampaign uses machine learning to automate email sequences, segment audiences, and personalize content based on user behavior.
- HubSpot: HubSpot offers AI-powered email marketing automation, including tools for lead nurturing, personalized content, and campaign analytics.

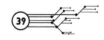

## AI Tools for Data Analytics and Insights

AI-driven analytics tools provide businesses with deeper insights into their campaigns, helping them make data-driven decisions. These tools analyze vast amounts of data quickly, allowing marketers to track performance and optimize strategies in real-time.

Popular AI analytics tools include:
- **Google Analytics with AI:** Google Analytics uses AI-powered insights to track website traffic, user behavior, and campaign performance, offering suggestions for optimization.
- **Tableau:** Tableau is an AI-powered data visualization tool that helps businesses understand their data through interactive, easy-to-read charts and dashboards.
- **Sisense:** Sisense uses AI to analyze complex data sets and generate actionable insights, helping businesses improve their decision-making and marketing strategies.

## Case Studies: Companies Successfully Using AI in Marketing

AI is no longer a futuristic concept—many companies are already leveraging AI tools to improve their digital marketing strategies.

Here are a few examples of businesses that have successfully integrated AI into their marketing efforts:
- **Coca-Cola:** Coca-Cola uses AI to analyze customer data, predict preferences, and create personalized marketing campaigns that resonate with individual consumers.
- **Netflix:** Netflix leverages AI to recommend personalized content to users based on their viewing history, leading to higher user engagement and satisfaction.
- **Amazon:** Amazon uses AI to power its recommendation engine, suggesting products based on customer browsing and purchase history, leading to increased sales.

These companies demonstrate the transformative power of AI in marketing, offering a glimpse into the future of AI-driven business success.

This chapter has explored some of the most powerful AI tools available to businesses, from content creation and social media management to customer service and advertising. While AI tools offer immense potential, choosing the right ones for your business can be daunting. If you need help navigating these tools, don't hesitate to consult an expert to ensure you're making the best decisions for your business.

# Chapter 10:
# The Future of
# Digital Marketing with AI

The impact of artificial intelligence (AI) on digital marketing is undeniable, and its influence is only set to grow. As businesses continue to adopt AI-driven tools and strategies, the future of digital marketing will be shaped by increasingly sophisticated technologies, offering deeper insights, greater personalization, and more efficient processes. This chapter will explore the emerging trends in AI for marketing and how businesses can prepare for the future.

## Emerging Trends in AI and Digital Marketing

AI is constantly evolving, and new technologies are emerging that will transform the digital marketing landscape even further. Here are some of the most exciting trends to watch:

- **Voice Search Optimization:** With the rise of virtual assistants like Alexa, Siri, and Google Assistant, voice search is becoming more prevalent. AI will play a crucial role in helping businesses optimize their content for voice search, ensuring that their products and services are discoverable when users speak their queries.
- **Visual Search:** AI-powered visual search tools, like those used by Pinterest and Google Lens, allow users to search for products using images rather than text. This shift presents an opportunity for businesses to optimize their product images for search engines, making it easier for consumers to find what they're looking for.
- **AI-Generated Content:** AI is already capable of creating written content, but the future will see even more sophisticated AI models capable of producing multimedia content, including videos, podcasts, and interactive experiences. This will allow businesses to scale their content production efforts significantly.
- **Hyper-Personalization:** As AI becomes better at analyzing data, businesses will be able to create hyper-personalized experiences for their customers. From customized emails to dynamic website content, AI will allow businesses to deliver exactly what each individual customer wants, in real-time.
- **AI-Driven Predictive Marketing:** AI will continue to improve its ability to predict customer behavior and trends, allowing marketers to anticipate what customers want before they even know it themselves. This will lead to more effective, proactive marketing strategies that drive higher engagement and conversions

**The Impact of Generative AI (ChatGPT, DALL-E, etc.)**

Generative AI, like the technology behind ChatGPT and DALL-E, is revolutionizing how businesses approach creativity and automation. These tools can generate content, images, and even video based on simple text inputs, allowing businesses to create custom marketing materials in minutes.

The impact of generative AI on digital marketing includes:
- **Content generation:** AI models like GPT-3 and GPT-4 can create human-like content that is optimized for SEO, email campaigns, and social media. This allows businesses to scale their content production quickly without sacrificing quality.
- **Visual creation:** AI tools like DALL-E enable businesses to generate unique images based on text descriptions, reducing the need for stock images and allowing for greater customization in marketing visuals.
- **Creative freedom:** Generative AI can be used to brainstorm new ideas, develop creative concepts, and even write scripts for advertisements or videos. This opens the door for more innovative marketing strategies without the usual resource constraints.

# Preparing for the Future with AI in Marketing

As AI continues to evolve, businesses must stay ahead of the curve by embracing AI-driven marketing strategies. Here are a few steps businesses can take to prepare for the future of AI in digital marketing:
1. **Invest in AI Tools:** Start by integrating AI-powered tools into your existing marketing efforts. Whether it's for content creation, social media management, or customer service, using AI tools now will help your business become more efficient and competitive in the long run.
2. **Focus on Data:** AI thrives on data, so businesses need to ensure they are collecting and analyzing customer data effectively. By understanding your audience better, AI tools can help you deliver more personalized and relevant marketing messages.

3. Stay Updated on Trends: The AI landscape is constantly changing, so it's essential to stay informed about the latest trends and technologies. Regularly evaluate new AI tools and strategies that can benefit your business and keep you ahead of the competition.
4. Maintain the Human Touch: While AI can automate many marketing processes, it's essential to maintain the human touch in your customer interactions. AI should enhance, not replace, the personal relationships you build with your customers.

(Note to the reader: As AI technology becomes more advanced, having a professional to guide you through this rapidly changing landscape is invaluable. If you need help preparing your business for the future of AI in digital marketing, feel free to reach out for expert assistance.)

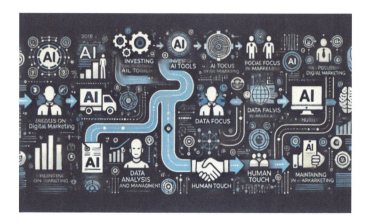

## Ethical Considerations in AI Marketing

As AI becomes more integrated into digital marketing, ethical considerations will also come to the forefront. Businesses must ensure they are using AI responsibly, particularly when it comes to data privacy, transparency, and fairness.
Key ethical considerations for AI in marketing include:

- Data privacy: Businesses must be transparent about how they collect and use customer data for AI-driven marketing efforts. Ensuring that customers understand and consent to data collection is crucial for maintaining trust.
- **AI transparency:** It's essential to disclose when AI is being used in customer interactions. For example, letting users know that they are chatting with a bot rather than a human ensures transparency and fosters a positive customer experience.
- **Bias and fairness:** AI systems can unintentionally reinforce biases based on the data they are trained on. Businesses should regularly audit their AI models to ensure they are fair and unbiased in their marketing efforts.

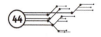

## Final Thoughts on the Future of AI in Digital Marketing

AI is undoubtedly shaping the future of digital marketing, enabling businesses to reach their customers in new and innovative ways. As AI tools become more advanced, they will continue to enhance every aspect of marketing, from content creation and personalization to customer service and advertising.

However, while AI can automate many processes, it's important to remember that the human element is still essential. As businesses prepare for the future, they should aim to combine the efficiency of AI with the creativity and empathy that only humans can provide.

By staying informed about AI trends, investing in the right tools, and ensuring ethical use, businesses can position themselves for success in the evolving digital marketing landscape.

This chapter explores the exciting future of digital marketing with AI, from emerging trends like voice and visual search to the impact of generative AI. As AI continues to evolve, businesses that embrace this technology will be well-positioned to thrive in the competitive digital landscape.
With this, we've covered the major areas where AI is transforming digital marketing. I hope this e-book has provided valuable insights and actionable steps for integrating AI into your marketing strategy

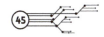

## Conclusion: Embracing AI for a Smarter Future in Digital Marketing

As we've explored throughout this e-book, artificial intelligence (AI) is revolutionizing digital marketing in profound ways. From automating time-consuming tasks to creating personalized content and providing deeper insights, AI offers businesses the tools they need to stay competitive in an increasingly complex and fast-paced digital landscape.

Key Takeaways

1. **AI Optimizes Efficiency:** One of AI's greatest strengths is its ability to streamline processes, from automating customer service with chatbots to optimizing ad campaigns and content creation. Businesses can achieve more with fewer resources, allowing them to focus on higher-level strategy and creativity.
2. **Personalization at Scale:** AI makes it possible to deliver hyper-personalized experiences that drive engagement and loyalty. Whether it's through tailored product recommendations, dynamic ads, or personalized email campaigns, AI allows businesses to connect with customers on a deeper level.
3. **Data-Driven Decision Making:** With AI, businesses can leverage data to make smarter, more informed decisions. AI tools analyze vast amounts of data in real-time, providing insights that help businesses optimize their strategies and stay ahead of the competition.
4. **The Future of Marketing is AI-Powered:** AI is here to stay, and its influence on digital marketing will only continue to grow. Businesses that embrace AI now will be better prepared to succeed in the future, as emerging technologies like voice search, visual search, and generative AI become more prevalent.

## Steps to Implement AI in Your Marketing Strategy

If you're ready to start integrating AI into your digital marketing efforts, here are some practical steps to follow:

1. **Identify Key Areas for AI Integration:** Consider which aspects of your marketing can benefit most from AI. Whether it's content creation, customer service, or advertising, start with the areas where AI can have the most immediate impact.
2. **Choose the Right Tools:** Select AI tools that align with your goals and needs. As covered in Chapter 9, there are many powerful AI tools available, so choose those that can streamline your processes and enhance your campaigns.
3. **Focus on Data:** Ensure you have a robust system in place for collecting and analyzing data. AI thrives on data, so the more you understand your audience, the better your AI-driven marketing efforts will perform.
4. **Maintain Ethical AI Practices:** Always ensure transparency in your AI-driven efforts, particularly when it comes to data privacy and customer interactions. Trust is a critical component of successful AI integration.
5. **Iterate and Improve:** AI is constantly evolving, and so should your marketing strategies. Regularly evaluate the performance of your AI tools and strategies, and make adjustments to stay ahead of the curve.

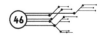

## Final Reflections

AI is transforming how businesses connect with their audiences, offering a smarter, faster, and more personalized approach to digital marketing. However, it's important to remember that AI is a tool, not a replacement for human creativity and strategy. The most successful marketing efforts will be those that combine the efficiency of AI with the ingenuity and emotional intelligence of human marketers.

As AI continues to advance, we're on the brink of a new era in digital marketing—one where businesses can not only automate processes but also deliver truly exceptional customer experiences. By embracing AI now, you position your business to thrive in this future, where marketing becomes more intelligent, intuitive, and impactful than ever before.

Thank you for taking the time to explore how AI can transform your business with digital marketing. I hope this e-book has provided you with the knowledge and tools you need to start leveraging AI in your marketing efforts. Remember, if you need help navigating the world of AI, I'm always here to assist you.

## Additional Resources

To help you continue exploring the world of AI and digital marketing, I've compiled a list of valuable resources. These tools, websites, and books will provide you with further insights and practical knowledge to successfully implement AI-driven strategies in your business.

### Books

1. "AI for Marketing and Product Innovation" by A. K. Pradeep, Andrew Appel, and Stan Sthanunathan
2. This book dives deep into how AI is transforming marketing and product innovation, offering insights into how businesses can use AI to drive growth.
3. "Artificial Intelligence in Marketing" by Katie King
4. Katie King provides a comprehensive guide on the role of AI in marketing, with practical examples and case studies from real-world applications.
5. "Prediction Machines: The Simple Economics of Artificial Intelligence" by Ajay Agrawal, Joshua Gans, and Avi Goldfarb
6. This book explores how AI is reshaping industries and offers valuable insights into how businesses can harness AI to improve decision-making and performance.

### Blogs and Websites

1. AI in Marketing Blog by Neil Patel
2. Neil Patel's blog covers a variety of topics related to AI in marketing, including automation tools, data analytics, and personalized marketing strategies.
3. Visit Neil Patel's Blog
4. HubSpot's AI in Marketing Hub
5. HubSpot offers in-depth guides, articles, and case studies on how AI is changing the marketing landscape, with practical advice on how to implement AI-driven tools in your strategy.
6. Explore HubSpot AI Hub
7. Marketing AI Institute
8. This website is a great resource for learning more about AI-powered marketing tools, trends, and best practices. It includes articles, case studies, and access to events focused on AI in marketing.
9. Visit Marketing AI Institute

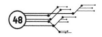

**AI Tools and Platforms**

1. OpenAI GPT-4
2. For content creation, GPT-4 by OpenAI is one of the most advanced language models available, capable of generating high-quality written content, answering queries, and assisting with creative processes.
3. Learn more about GPT-4
4. Hootsuite
5. Hootsuite's AI-powered social media management tool helps businesses schedule posts, track engagement, and optimize social media strategies for better results.
6. Visit Hootsuite
7. Mailchimp
8. This AI-powered email marketing platform offers advanced segmentation, personalized content recommendations, and performance analytics, helping businesses run more effective email campaigns.
9. Visit Mailchimp
10. Tableau
11. Tableau is a leading AI-powered data visualization tool that helps businesses analyze and present data in clear, interactive dashboards, providing insights to inform marketing strategies.
12. Visit Tableau

## Courses and Certifications

1. AI for Everyone by Andrew Ng (Coursera)
2. This course offers an excellent introduction to AI, making it accessible to non-technical professionals who want to understand how AI can impact their business.
3. AI for Everyone Course
4. HubSpot Academy: AI in Marketing
5. HubSpot Academy offers free courses that teach the fundamentals of AI in marketing, covering everything from automation tools to predictive analytics.
6. HubSpot Academy AI Course
7. AI in Digital Marketing by Udemy
8. This Udemy course provides a comprehensive overview of how AI is used in digital marketing, including practical applications and case studies.
9. AI in Digital Marketing Course

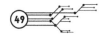